t2

Watermarks

Phil Kirby

Hope you enjoy it.

Ri...

7/9/11

arrowhead
poetry

First published 2009 by
Arrowhead Press
70 Clifton Road, Darlington
Co. Durham, DL1 5DX
Tel: (01325) 260741

Typeset in 10 on 14pt Laurentian by
Arrowhead Press

Email: editor@arrowheadpress.co.uk
Website: http://www.arrowheadpress.co.uk

ISBN 978-1-904852-24-7

Printed in Great Britain by the MPG Books Group, Bodmin and King's Lynn

To all my family – the late and the living
especially to Jenny and Beth – as always

Acknowledgements

Acknowledgements are due to the editors of the following magazines in which many of these poems, or versions of them, first appeared: *Critical Survey, Envoi, Interpreter's House, London Magazine, nthposition, Other Poetry, Poetry & Audience, Poetry Digest, Seam, Smiths Knoll and The Frogmore Papers.*

Several poems have also previously appeared in the following pamphlets: *Third Person Gossip* and *Of Silent Houses* (both Waldean Press) and *A Bowl of Sky* (Shoestring Press).

Jacket Photograph:

Watermarks
© 2009 Phil Kirby

Author's Notes

The *Stories from Hopper* poems are ideas suggested by the paintings whose titles they bear and are intended as a kind of sequence, though the paintings themselves are not.

A Perfect Wife was written after hearing the extraordinary true story of a Japanese woman who sacrificed herself and her children in order that her husband would have no family ties to prevent him becoming an honourable Kamikaze pilot.

Contents

Labyrinth

A door opens. Thought, like Theseus,
moves towards a fissured labyrinth,
but twine-less and wandering;
searching for an untouched heart,
the pure white clay of life,
awaiting shape and hoping to be fired.

But the winding path deceives,
its walls daubed with prints – hands, fingers,
widening loops and whorls of influence.
Questions span the threshold.
Outside, rolling days are clear;
bright skies bustle with birds and futures.

The Carpenter's Workshop

Our father spent long evenings there,
shuffling through scobs heaped around his feet,
his face yellow under oil-lamps,
eyes straining at the angles of his sharpened blades.

Against one wall he set completed frames.
Sometimes I rocked them on the uneven flags,
playing with the balance,
feeling the shift of their weight.

Even now I miss the sound of tools at work;
the smell, sometimes sweet as nectarines,
of sap and resin seeping from the grain;
and scented wood-chips gathered in loose clothing.

Such beautiful hands, one neighbour said.
He couldn't bear to knock or cut them.
On good days, he would lift me high
onto his shoulders and I would know his strength.

Grandmother

We are sitting on a home-made rocking-horse
that my father, your son-in-law, fashioned
from the off-cuts of his vehicle trade.

Your face is creased, like comfortable leather,
below rolls of dark hair. Natural? Or did I see
a headscarf knotted at the front, plastic curlers?

That cardigan – lilac or grey? – black skirt
and a floral pinny that could never
have looked right outside the sixties.

It was the sadness of others that wrung tears
from me when you died. I didn't understand,
didn't know what you being dead really meant.

I'd seen you earlier that day in your room; saw
the walnut bed-end, the candlewick bed-spread;
felt the silence like rustling silk. I still can't see your face.

I know you must have left me more than these
pictures: perhaps there was some traveller in
your bronze skin that's often made me restless.

Grandson four arrived the next February, England
won the World Cup not long after, and somehow
that's become important. I can name the German team,

recall the commentary, see men on the pitch,
their timing wrong: "They think it's all over...It is now!"
Your arm is round me and I don't know how it felt.

The Real World

A butterfly, broken and tumbling
across our summer windscreen
and dropping, suddenly inert, like paper,
is not a symbol of destruction
or the ruthlessness of progress;

and the wild flowers we crushed
by accident beneath our booted feet –
petal colours bruised to the sap –
do not represent the disconnection
of man from his surroundings.

Nor do pheasants, or hares, hung
in rows on butcher's hooks –
still soft, half-eyed, crimson beads
congealing at their open mouths –
illustrate our savage history.

This grey drizzle falling, blurring
lines between the land and sky,
un-defining distances and detail,
is no reflection of a mood;
is no 'pathetic fallacy'.

That car half-buried, one shoe
nearby, last-gasping in the muddy ooze,
is not a modern metaphor
for hopelessness, the ash and dust
of how things end,

just as the leather-faced couple
we saw beneath the grease and grime-
dulled wall-lights in a bar – no word
or look, going home to sleep apart –
say nothing special about loneliness.

But your tools, the worn and unworn
clothes we'll have to throw away,
the books you read, the untouched scotch –
all these convey the sense, the knowledge,
the simple fact that you are gone.

Memento

This face, these hands, at once
familiar and strange as landscapes,
passed on to me for safe keeping.
I wore them every day, thinking somehow
we'd be connected still, or something
closer, more immediate, would be maintained.
The only thing I noticed was that time
became more precious for a month or two.

Not just how uselessly or well it filled,
but the very keeping of it, checking
what was lost or gained. The morning

we pulled his watch from my pocket,
machine-washed, stilled forever,
for a second it was like he'd gone again.

His Green Chair

There, among white lupins, sits
the cricket ball we found in a tree
on that playing field in Winchmore Hill.
Matt and scuffed but still bright red,
it's almost come to mean that day:
the wind lifting your gliders so high
we thought they'd be blown to the Thames;
crimson handled tools – for fine adjustments –
showing from your pocket;
cars, always, on that main road;
and players shouting from a football pitch.
When the sun went, so did we, back
for lunch – something cold, fresh bread;
new flowers in an almost cut-glass vase.
After, you dozed in the stiff green armchair
which then was yours and yours alone.

Today there's cricket on T.V.
When I settle down to watch it
I won't be in your chair.
It's been with me for years and still
it's shaped to how you used to sit.

Photograph: 1962

Recognise him? Yes, I think so.
Yes, it's in the eyes. They are
the only thing that seems
to look at all familiar about
the boy who, with arms folded,
trilby hat and pipe stuck in
the corner of his stiff-lipped mouth,
stands posed as Maigret on the doorstep.

Something in the black and whiteness
of the photograph, its capturing
of age – his innocence, that shirt –
which like a shutter flicker-
flacks across my thoughts, keeps me
so far from really seeing him,
I'm left to wonder if he dreamt of me
the way I dream of him now.

The Wasps' Nest

Knowing his wife treasures such objects
his mother gives a present: the beginnings
of a wasps' nest, coloured like dried dung.

Cupped in his trembling awkward hands
it is almost weightless; so fragile
the gentlest press would reduce it to bran.

Fashioned from the chew of wood and spit,
shapes and patterns repeat themselves,
one inside another. The dark blur curling

at its centre sharpens into sudden images
he can't black out: a bungalow; one apple
on a sapling; thick-scented rose buds

unfurling; the boy whose blunted knife
beheads a wasp felled in the bathroom,
the gritty execution appalling in its thrill.

The Way She Is

Her fears describe it best:
the dislike of tube trains; panic
as birds or moths come fluttering close;
the ugliness of insects, the threat of frogs;
the fact that she can drive
but never does these days.
And all the things she 'hates'.

It's in the plainness of her dresses,
the natural colour of her hair,
the one bag and Tweed perfume;
a new-found love of fuchsias
and the time to tend them;
the way she laughs and holds herself
in pain, not saying why or finding out.

Mostly now I see things from the distance
between her and what I've become.

Through Robert's Window

Looking through the open window
sounds that once meant home combine
with sunlight on walls and flowers,
to re-create things half-forgotten:

white points of sun on jets
scoring arcs across clear sky;
wind through trees above
a bird-box, hopeless in delphiniums;
the mower in my mother's hands,
the strokes I could never master.

But this childless place, this view,
these empty gardens, are no longer mine.
I shut them out; think of our father's quiet,
the host of things unspoken.

A Gardener's Tale

Another beginning.
I have dug the dark soil,
burned groundsel and milkweed.
There is earth beneath my nails.

Now I rest on the spade,
think about the beauty of flowers;
about what has grown and gone
and what may come again.

I know her dislike of carnations,
remember that sickly bunch
in a jug but not in water;
and how long the bottled orchids lasted.

So this time I will start with
one blue iris in a plain white vase,
with ladder ferns and ivy;
then fill her rooms with freesias.

And when their scent has gone
we will walk around her garden
between the trees I mean to plant –
walnut, hazel and cherry –

and I will make a pledge to her:
to always remember this feeling,
this sense of starting over,
until they first bear fruit.

In His Image

Among the trailing plants, a pot:
the head of some Greek god, maybe,
impassive, strong – but sad. At least
something in its look suggesting loss,
though there are no lines or furrows.
Groomed ringlets, moustache and beard
lend an age denied by its smooth cheeks.
It is his eyes, so blank,
as if the tears had all been cried,
that draw me down to look and wonder
in whose image he was made.
I lift his cold face up to mine, sense
the weight of fired earth; the emptiness.
I look around the nursery to see
what beauty could be planted in this head.

'Beata Beatrix'

No, not a halo. But something
glows there, around you. Something
that has often made me stare,
or watch you just sitting.

I think you must have seen me
turn away almost ashamed, embarrassed
like a school-boy being caught,
betrayed by guilty looks.

And then some music becomes you,
your tumbling hair and dark eyes closing;
the shapes you've made against the light;
the haunting pictures painted in my head.

I would offer this, hoping it could stop
the red bird laying poppies in your hand.

Stories from Hopper #1

'Summertime, 1943'

She holds the cold stone,
leans gently on the portico –
facing a breeze that pushes through
curtains into an unlit room – as if
searching out the flags of summer;
dressed to feel its warmth: straw hat
and short-sleeved frock, thin
against her leading thigh.

She has stepped into slanting light,
released from the darkness of the hall,
from all that's pressed her
into ways she cannot bear.

This season. This will be the one,
she thinks, and starts to plan
the contents of a leather case,
which sits unused beneath her bed.

Her eyes betray no feeling as
she composes in her head the note
she'll leave against the salt pot;
imagines how he'll shout and rage
in empty rooms at all the things
she's left behind, that still mean her
but only say how much she hated him.

A Perfect Wife

My love, I have packed away our things.
The cherry is in bloom; your favourite
carp – mirrored, huge, and somehow buoyant –
are fed and basking, sculling under waterfalls.

In your absence, I have studied
how to be a perfect wife: careful, silent
hands sliding back the paper screens;
making tea like one of Utamaro's women.

The children both are peaceful now.
When I join them, and we sleep together,
I hope our dreams will be of wings
and what your final flight will bring:

you home, divine, bright with glory, carrying
our names upon a banner dressed with prayers.

Elsewhere in Wimbledon

So often it comes down to this:
an aimless competition when the court is empty,
labouring to score some useless points
from one another's failings, or small faults,
still hoping to play out the match
and end with something left to love.

Battle

April under leaden skies.
Sounds of rain; cars on wet roads.
Irregular ticking drips from trees
unsettle my sense of time.

On plastic maps, opposing forces are
in red and blue. I un-pick Normans
from the tapestry, picture chain mail
hidden by this haze and grey light.

Harold's housecarls marched
from York to London, then here,
unsure of the future. Tired bodies
taut with fear, they somehow

forged a will to fight, thinking
only to protect their cherished things
from invasions of the outside world.
Now, we know the battle was lost.

The losers did not write history.
Opposers of the new are not remembered
for themselves, but for their stand
against what seems to us inevitable.

On salty winds, something unfurls
above the abbey walls: the banner of change,
coloured by opposing forces –
by the heat of success, the cold of failure.

Separation

For now, their house alone has ears
for the sounds of her absence
and a hoarse clamouring of crows
through an open fan-light. His view
of other birds across the lawn
and field serves to contract
what comfort he gets from walls.
Heat focuses through the window
onto his blank face. He is silent,
momentarily hemmed-in by spaces,
knowing any words would shock
only the room and be pointless.

A Mouthful of Lark

'They used to eat skylarks,' he said.
'Maybe thirty thousand a year.'
And he said they are rarer now, even in spring
when above meadows and wheat
the air seems so laced with their singing
just to breathe it in could make us high.

But this is autumn.
Starlings gather on a weather-vane.
One dead tree is filled with rooks.
By a field of stubble,
someone stops for directions.
In the almost-silence
after she drives away
I look up, listen to the absence,
and for a moment try to imagine
a mouthful of lark – its texture
and taste on my tongue;
the feeling of having its song
in my throat.

Flame Season

Trains clatter against a bowl of sky.
Among trees and long shadows
I am lodging in an autumn city.
Magpies settle on a chain-link fence
where gathered leaves give scent
to days so doused with dew
they could be an attempt
to stop the coming flame season.

Sunday bells ring clear above
ripe fields; thorny hedges drip
crimson berries: reminders of God.
But I have put my faith in us
and how these evenings thicken
in the woods like bonfire smoke.

The day descends

to a dome of light above the square
half-filled with kids and fast cars.
Along the street

a boy says goodnight to a girl
then runs off in that way
you know means he's in love.

Beyond him, distant streetlamps
strung across the dark,
warm colours through drawn curtains

that make me think of you,
legs curled in an armchair
that's always been too small.

Cold wind drums my tightened face.
Its sound fills my ears
and suddenly I feel like running.

Epithalamium
(for D&D)

To take these elements, the stuff
of worlds, of suns, the universe;
the origins of all we've been,
and are, and know – to take all this
and step once more up to the flame
with more than hope; with certainty
that any imperfections, marks
or dents will not resist the forge.

To heat them. Next, to listen for
the hammer, and the anvil's song,
then watch the sudden sparks as, blow
by blow, a precious thing takes shape:
two elements combined and changed
to make this gentle glow – this ring.

The Fascination of Fire

I drive through smoke –
smells of wood and paper burning –
and in those moments while the sun is blurred
I think of you in winter, at the hearth
twisting ribbons of yesterday's news,
arranging them beneath kindling,
then laying on applewood logs;

or outside building sticks into a heap
of such a shape that, when it's lit, you are
staring at a stook of fire, its unsteady light
animating shadows on your face.
Drawn from the flames by your movement,
I watch you come back in, anticipate
an acrid perfume on your clothes and hair.

A Time When

There may be a time
when one look
will set the fields on fire
and dry, blonde wheat turn
powder black.

There may be a time
when one word
will set an eager crowd alight,
clamouring to acclaim,
short of breath.

There may be a time
when one touch
will turn some lover's soul to gold,
all resistance melted,
soft, precious.

There will be a time
when, one day,
this tower of babble falls into place
and all your thoughts
become clear.

For now, your father
must remain
frustrated, a little saddened, until
you acquire a voice and
learn to speak.

Routine Journey With Thirty-Five Trucks

At home:

      from our window there is thick mist.
      The world dissolves beyond the garden.
      Trees make coral shapes against the brightness;
      one light hovers in a pale silhouette:
      the geometry of backstreet rooftops.

Driving to work:

      I discover a dislike for the taste of lipstick.
      A capped man leans against the gate
      of a field where mist is losing out to the sun.
      It's the best of anything he'd be likely
      to see there, but he's reading stars.

At work:

      some things sink in, others don't.
      These days it feels like circus training,
      just so much jumping through hoops.
      Ironic that the cage offers securities
      it's hard to abandon, for all my jungle dreams.

On the way back from work:

      stopped by the only level-crossing for miles,
      I speculate as to the sound of God's laughter.
      Thirty-five trucks pass, peaked with coal.
      I think of horses grazing tethered on the roadside;
      I think of open fields.

At home:

      you are in front of the telly. A handful
      of un-opened junk mail is on the ironing board.
      Your coffee's gone cold, as usual
      and it seems as if it's always been like this, as if
      nothing has happened today. Perhaps nothing has.

Three Months On

He comes in unannounced and stands
at my shoulder, watching as I return
cheap cutlery to its drawer, reciting
in my head the drilled-in list he learned
on National Service: knife, fork, spoon –
but no tin mug.
                         And there the moment
breaks. It feels like breathing out,
and he is gone until recalled,
maybe by the corkless bottle-stopper
hiding on the shelf. When I found you
that morning, crying, it was little things,
you said, that 'got you'. They get us
less and less these days – most recently
Sinatra, singing *You Will Be My Music*.
One day soon I'll frame a photograph.

Measurement

There is no horizon. Only fragile minds
struggling from their shells of bone
impose such limitations on this slow-bent blue;
create tomorrows when there are none.

The cold-moon-sway of curling sea is far
outside our measure, beyond what's known
as time. Its glassy roll shattered on rocks
long before we hunted down and trapped the sun.

Now the ink of evening stains the sky.
Lights from distant oil-rigs jump and flicker,
bounce over waves like bright stones skimming
towards an almost empty shore. A father

and child, confined by limits on their days
leave marks in wet sand – names, a face –
one knowing how the endless breath of tides
will make them disappear without a trace.

'And it comes...'

On some days
it's in contours of ragged clouds,
the way they change familiar skylines.
Others, it may be
dark waters of a lake
enamelled by a glaring sun;
or noises of the wind like cartoon ghosts
through our windows.
And it comes in the way
this early honey-warmth sags and oozes
golden, slow and cautious
as a tide's edge on the sand:

just once to do something memorable
and still be living –
not piled up on monuments
with names of the fallen.

Of Dabs and Dogfish

There were people riding horses on the beach.
Mud-flats, she said, so flat
the wind might have been a jack-plane.

I went to stand alone at the water's edge,
watched it spilling towards the creek
where we'd seen the scatter of a thousand dogfish-fry;
a two-inch dab, dead and drying
in the long uncovered hours
between tides we never saw come in.
Our timing can be laughable.

Darkness slowly settled on the rim of land.
From the far shore, lights and wood smoke
struggled over empty beaches.
I could not name what was wrong
until, swept back by the night
to our caravan beneath the stars,
to her so gently drawn by gaz-light,
she asked was I communing with my spirit.

I nodded vacantly;
heard myself describe a wish
to live in higher places.

What We Have Come To

It's pointless wishing this street
was called something 'Boulevard'
or hoping with closed eyes, sun
warming our faces, that we could
be transported to an amazing beach
in California. This house, this town
is where we are and no-one
could blame a stranger for believing
this is what we have come to:
detachment, space, the bills paid
monthly and a sense of comfort.
The colours you look good in

have changed; grown more numerous
at least. As we are hurled along
the motorway, December light slopes
across us, stretching shadow-vehicles
to the ridiculous. Cars and high banks
under a clear sky. Everyone but us
is having two kids, it seems. The talk
comes round to that and it feels
like summer briefly, but for
the stiff-laced trees binding windless
fields. We can cry even now for
all the things remaining unresolved.

Another Jericho

There were tears, of course. On both sides.
Strangers held hands through gaps, seized moments
as the sounding brass of change
played revolution at all Europe's feet.
Walls fell like applause;
laughter slipped between the wires;
birds' wings spread in clearer skies.

That same year, in a syrupy warmth,
our daughter's innocence breached another wall:
"Where is the baby that you lost?"
Answerless, you moved quietly
into a different room,
stood in sunlight by the window,
crying for another fallen Jericho.

For An Only Child

The last one in the box has done its job.
Now a wait, until the tucked away vermilion
spreads over coals heaped in the dark grate.
In an hour, perhaps, the room will warm.
By the time I go to fetch her
I'll have fed the fire again.

As glowing schoolrooms gather dusk about them,
amid hellos and smiles to mums and minders
I'll do her zip, tie a lace or two
and ask about her day. She will say
she can't remember what she's done,
that so-and-so has lost the ribbon from her hair,
at lunch-time someone kicked a ball into the beck
and can she have some sweets.

Then coming home, we will race for the door
and I shall lose. When she sits to watch t.v.
and switches off, content inside her own expanding world,
she will feel the warmth but not really see the fire
or how I've shaped the room to comfort her.

Sky in Winter

Like a long split in the belly of a salmon
a keen glass edge of frosted air
cuts through clouds to reveal
a blushing sun, caught in the act
of keeping someone else warm.

Of Wonder and Light

It was cold that night, so cold.
I could see the feeble lights of houses
gathered into villages; traced lines
of roads that led towards the little town
where He was born some days before.
I tried so hard to light the way,
and though they'd seen, and followed,
I felt so pale, so small – unchosen;
just one of all those millions. I'd wanted
to smell fresh straw, to hear from stalls
the gentle sounds of animals; be warmed by
the glow which I knew had filled the stable
when all were gathered there; to see
her face just once, be blessed by her smile.
I never heard the first cry; or saw the gifts.
I was too high up. And cold.

I left them there and turned away,
aware that it was almost dawn.

Promise

This is how his day begins: she says
a cockerel keeps on waking her at three or four,
that then it's hard to stop herself from getting up
and she wishes the weather would break.
She leaves for work; he watches her drive away.
For a while the road is empty. Then comes noise,
a gathering stream of other cars, maybe a tractor.
At 7:25 a bus arrives and waits.

Then breakfast; someone calling 'Sheila';
some gesture with housework and a coming back
to questions, like how, when they set out
in that summer of dogs on a hill,
they could have got like this: lives almost apart,
barely a deliberate touch, routines to set watches by;
and how, when he thinks back to the boy who looked out
on bright roads, houses and un-opened doors,
he has become this man, set against flat landscapes
with splintered fences and ivy binding ragged barns;
with cola tins on the slow canal, the river in flood.

Then, As Now

Again it comes to this:
time sliding by unaccounted for;
sun kneading landscapes into warmer shapes;
pictures from the past when,
as we got off the train,
a building was in flames.

Somewhere round these city streets
a siren plies its warning.
It seems there must be anguish,
someone's eyes unsure,
well-thumbed plans in shreds;
dreams in pieces round a shot-gun butt.

Once in our old street a siege was on,
roads blocked, mouths open, telling how
he'd waited till the family went out.
Local kids were high on thrill.
I felt it, too, seeing armed policemen
crouched at his rear fence.

Our house was empty
but for dust in squares of light.
Evening pressed against the outside walls.
I waited for you then, as now, cautious,
uncertain of the closing day,
vacant minutes filling with false alarm.

Overture

Where we live, it's April.
Outside, a longed-for lighter evening
sets down behind the other side of town
and draws us into such cold air
it's surely flattered by this cloudless sky.

Passing backroads you say
you haven't walked in all these years,
we're prompted to a list of reasons why
you'd like this one to start again
and try to count our luck. But

a sense of what that means
evades us – as all colour starts to fail
and a brazen finch, concealed within this
trembling blossom, startles with its urgent song
repeating in the day's last throes.

A Bamboo Tent

She binds a bamboo tent with twine,
secures some stiffer netting. Her digging
chimes against the glass of windows
as she turns the earth, prepares
shallow drills, thumbs-in tiny seeds.
Another season begins like this
in a cool expanse of evening.

By some rosemary, flowering
rain-cloud blue, she watches
her daughter tend imaginary plants;
wonders how it might have been
if things had not gone wrong, if all
loose ends of expectation had been tied.
Again she bends, to smooth the bed.

Something We Never Meant

Our mistake has brought about
an accidental ending. Coming home,
knowing she won't be there,
things along the road assume a new importance:

rows of bone-white stalks in rich brown fields;
a timber cross on a ragged heap of twigs;
the travellers' camp by the railway line deserted,
yellow grass where the caravans stood.

Dusk falls. Beyond a hedge signals change
and I don't know what they mean –
if the train that's on its way is
heading North or South; full or empty.

It passes: two carriages,
warm light falling onto vacant seats,
the driver, going somewhere planned,
alone and in the dark.

Pastorale

There, in the sloping field
where ragged plastic banners, white and blue,
herald something starting
and try to snap the birds away;

that man passing, one fist full
of fresh-killed rabbits which, still lithe,
so newly dead, swing and falter
and hang to his rhythm –

there, a hundred rooks take flight,
rising over sunlit rails that slither
towards the power-station,
because a coal train hauls its weight

and passes, the wince of its wheels
keen along the shuddering paddocks
where one horse, unmoved, still grazes
and never once looks up.

Whatever Stays

Years away, years like dried-up fruits
we never quite get round to eating,
I will come down to earth. After all
the fears that clenched my stomach
to a helpless fist, be sure of only this.
Maybe, then, you'll read my work,
wonder if it should be kept; tell your kids
how grandad worked wood, taught,
or butterflied much of the time he craved.

It would be nice to leave you
more than debts, or unjust duties:
the Africana and bric-a-brac I always hoped
would be worth something more than sentiment –
my records, perhaps.
These days you'd have to sell the house.
But these are only things.
It's hard to say if they last longer
than our words and actions and feelings.

Whatever stays, the ark of your memory
will rescue fragments of my life
and set them down in a quiet time
when the flood of the world subsides:
as stories passed on at Christmas tables
to family so young they never knew me;
who have only seen the photo albums
dating back to God-knows when,
the colour pictures showing other signs of age.

I hope what's left says what I could not.
While I've the chance I'll spare you all I can,
but your recollections could become
more precious than the life they recall.
Things I taught you may survive intact.
The magnolia tree or wisteria
I've always aimed at planting
will be in bloom by then.
Think of those flowers as my flag.

Stories from Hopper #2

'Pennsylvania Coal Town, 1947'

Cut grass and sulphur. The mix
is borne on warm air up the slopes,
making him pause, still the rake,
look valley-wards, momentarily lost
in unspecific thoughts of children's carts
and sunlight on the sides of houses.

With cut grass swept towards the urn's
red earthenware glow, its bent
plumage of leaves, he thinks of summers
in his homeland hills, could be
a million worlds from here; of woods
and cheese and bread on chequered cloths.

Now sulphur. Now chimneys, pitheads,
wheels turning silently – until the wind
brings their complaint to settle on lawns –
are grey silhouettes in near distance.
He knows the shifts, can time these weekends
by hooters and echoes; cut grass and sulphur.

Windfalls

It's been weeks. Our apples have sat
slowly burning in what pale sun late
October manages, like rounded embers.
Odd ones are the shape of open mouths.
We go out, my daughter and I, to rake
them up under a dull aluminium sky
tainted with smoke and sulphur – the way
it is round here when the clocks go back –
hoping all that falls on us is darkness,
which slowly purples distant hills.

She wants some for the pick-up on her trike.
The rest are wheelbarrow-bound. A barrow
of drum-skinned apples. Ripe-fleshed
fruit wasting naturally on the compost.
Blue half-light hides a sliver of guilt.
So much waste. Shapes of open mouths.

October

We'll make him six foot one, if that's okay –
a little more than me. In metric, though.

His hair will be my mousey brown, but thick
like yours, your dad's – we'll have him keep all his.

And let's imagine we have passed things on:
salt-watered blood that draws him to the sea;

a love of trees, of hills; a passion for
the sun-sweet-musted scent of forest floors.

His talents will include a flair for art –
a sensitivity to colour, line –

and sport. He'll love to sprint on late night roads
for no-one, nothing but the thrill of speed.

His hand and eye, his jaw, will just achieve
a handsomeness, a winning smile; that look.

He'll have a sharpened humour, naturally –
his older sister's wit will be his strop.

And yes, the two may sometimes fight or flounce,
slam doors to music neither of us likes,

but that's the price you pay with any kids:
you help them up, then teach yourself the art

of letting go. Just as we must with this
imagined boy who ghosts through autumn days

like these, in which we're walking sunlit fields,
describing him as if he *had* been born

and guessing what he might have asked for on
his list – he would have been fourteen this month.

What It Takes

Not that red car flashing down
through yellow fields; the windmill,
white and slowly turning beneath
a power station's pall of smoke and steam;

nor the fighter jets
that shake this metal sheet of sky
and leave a numbing silence in their wake,
or kestrels swooping into woods;

and it's not how atmospherics change
the sound of trains – one day roaring,
next day mute – or hidden, unknown birds
surprise our silver birch with song.

No. It's none of these, but something
at once so simple and so hard to understand:
a mother and her child; the knowledge that
had things gone her way there would be two.

Still Waters

They are three alone upon the river,
lapped timber sounding, like a drum,
with every bump and knock of oar,
with every plash and pull and lift;
him sensing through the blade and shaft

the soft resistance, each nuance of flow
and thrust, not even hearing
his wife's comments on how well he rows,
the underbreath of pleasure and surprise.
Something else is in his ears and eyes:

thirty years ago – another boat,
home-made; a boy who faces back
still trailing rod and float
in hope of mullet, while his father
rows against the sudden weather –

a quickening wind, storm clouds,
cold spray from ragged waves,
the beach no nearer; no other sounds
but the slap of sea on hull,
wind, and breathing – hard, fearful –

from a face trying to show calm.
Like this river now, their polished wake
slowly bending to the dam.
Today their daughter
leans over, hand in the water,

fingers open, as if at any moment
she might grab a bright-eyed fish,
snatch it from its element
and expose it to the glare
of daylight; to the dangers of air.

A New Tartarus

It is morning.

> Between sunlight-buttered walls
> of silent houses
> shards of birdsong
> pierce the shade or
> glint from telephone wires.

A wind hisses through leaves.

> Curtains draw on the new Tartarus.
> The flaming wheel of the sun
> turns again on its prisoners,
> who bow to their desires only
> to find things have moved away.

Darkness folds into the clouds.

> No longer enthralled by myths
> an image of god still has
> to roll his stone from the garage
> and work his way
> to the summit of his sphere.

A storm begins to break.

Storms

We parted with the angry sky
flickering like candles in a tent.
A distant storm ranted wordless,
its sound soaked up by hills
and fields and far-off homes.

I stopped the car, got out
to watch, fresh-sighted. I felt
no rain, only the rush of wind.
Heavy clouds swelled like balloons
filled with the collapse of thunder.

The landscape jumped then froze
a moment, like a silent film.
I waited as the tension rang for
some needle-point to burst the skin
and let the storm come tumbling out.

Frost

Too many people get hung up about
the plainest things, like losing hair or weight
or awful weather; petty things compared
to sex and all the ego-crushing blows
dealt out in that cold war. No wind that whips
and rattles round the panes will ever be
as chill as vacant air between a man
and woman in a bed when careless thought
or thoughtless touch lets in the frost which both
could thaw if they but had the words enough.

Parting Shot

We never said a thing that mattered.
Just so much chatter – idle, senseless –
filling time until we hit on something
we hoped would really sting. We never did.

Dry leaves skittered round the wooden shelter;
someone's chimney billowed acrid smoke
that choked us speechless for two minutes,
then the almost empty bus arrived. And you got on.

This Long Lawn of Days

Last night I liked it here:
honeyed jazz oozing from a tape,
a rumbling wind through trees
that bass-drum-tumbled down
our chimney like broken sound,
falling at the wound-up whirr
of your sewing machine.
Even my pale hands getting bored
in the washing-up seemed okay.

But this long lawn of days
will never cut the same way twice
and what yesterday looked so green
soon gets trampled underfoot, or fades.
That's why tonight, in a pause,
while furious rain spits and spatters,
I want to pack my dreams
in a walnut shell and wait
till someone moves a river to my door.

Stories from Hopper #3

'Western Hotel'

I have been here many times before.
Something about the view, its bleakness;
something about how warmth falls in
through each expansive window.

My husband bought the dress. Crimson
suited me, he said, gave me such an air
of class on evenings when he took me
out. He liked to show me off.

It's stained a little now. I know
it's there, but you would never see –
only in a certain light, from such an angle:
the red wine he once threw.

I always bring this picture, too:
the kids, when they were three and five.
My favourite, now they're grown and gone.
Their smiling comforts me some days.

When the bottle-shiny green cab leaves,
I'll be alone. The whole motel to me
and staff; like the copper-faced imported
maid who showed me to the room.

I'll unpack soon. The silk
will need to hang. I don't know why
I left address tags on the handles.
They won't be going back.

And nor will I. Not this time.
I'd rather watch this empty road,
survey the empty hills, the quiet sky,
than sit at home and wait

all day for nothing to happen
so seriously; all night to hear a word
that might mean something new;
forever for a touch to say he's sorry.

The Backs of His Hands

Every day he hears the liquid throats of birds,
opens the curtains and wishes he could fly.
He checks the freckle-brown patterns on his hands
for signs of change, recounts every scar,
then sits for hours among his fallen years,
watching the sad parade of all he never was.

Sometimes nasturtiums come to mind,
or crimson sails; or Valerie, fourteen,
braced and tanned, laying back against a dune;
the broken promises of letters;
and in those moments he is young again,
music through the long summer twilights,
love at the garden gate, a first time for everything
and forever with the long forgotten school friends.

When night comes, so dark
it could be his whole life is contained
in the untidy living-room – its pile of local papers,
empty grate and coffee mug sticking to a faded table –
he pulls the curtains closed, climbs the stairs,
and feels again the hope of wings.

The Possibility of Loss

Shafts of 'miracle' fall solid on a hill.
Two geese beat the air that thickens
briefly into darkness at the door. Inside
she is waiting, seated at the bar, picked out
by more than just the space around her.

Words begin to edge around their fears;
stumble on the block of naming them.
Their eyes meet, turn from sudden awkwardness.
But a shadow alters their expressions
and it passes – she tells him she is resigned

to new horizons, accepts uncertain prospects;
will map her future differently.
While others gauge the weight of living
against the possibility of loss, today
what hope she has is shining like gold-leaf.

Gift

He can – with one hand – catch the sun,
control the shift from dark to light,

or gather up a starlit sky
to roll it out when most required,

no more than he can throw a cup
to hold the seas, or net the winds

that bring her voice, her scent; or find
within his gift the power to calm

her fears; a touch, some words – just
something that would stop her tears.

No Flowers

The flowers are gone.
After all this time, a year or more,
the public grief of those unknown bereaved
has found a quieter place to rest; a place
more private than this busy road-side verge,
buried under drifts of cow parsley.

I passed them every day;
noted when they'd been renewed.
But only now, in their absence,
does the grasping of another's loss
ream out the brass bell of my own insides
and make it sound a purer note.

Seeing the Light

After screens of trees
the country opens like a map,
mist smoothed out to the edge of visibility.
The flag of afternoon is flying
over sun-pervaded hills and distant water,
while I drive home to you, thinking
of the year when I was eight and didn't know
the world had things that could be changed;
thinking of a time when simple things amazed us –
like the winter someone drove their car
across the frozen lake.

A fan of shadows flickers on my face.
Now I am driving home to meet you.
We will sort things out
beneath the street-lamps sparking-up,
by the yard where steam rises into pink floodlights.
As once before, you will half laugh
and wonder if the flowers I bring
could mean that there is someone else.

Reunion

They arrive apart, at different times –
her with the child and car, him later
in plain leathers on the kind of bike
he dreamt of having twenty years ago –

for the weekend we've had planned for months.
Not all the friends have come. Some can't
because of lonely fathers; work. Others, perhaps,
we didn't really want. One was not invited.

It's just the way we've grown; much has changed –
we all have kids. Their voices drift in
from the garden where everyone is sitting
in the shade of trees, waiting for lunch.

I'm unsure if they all know about these two,
if they've been told how things have broken up.
It doesn't show, so great is her refusal
to accept the other life he's taken on.

In the dining room he quietly hands me
a photograph – his new partner, so different
from his wife – and I'm not sure what to say.
As I try to read her face, he stands by our dresser,

looks closely at the dried seahorse and starfish,
the tumbler full of shells, the clear glass jug
tucked behind a sickly plant; asks me why
we went for yellow walls. Handing back his secret,

we step outside, sunlight showing up his grey,
and hers. It's almost as if nothing's changed,
their curly little girl watching bees disappearing
into the mouths of crimson antirrhinums.

True Love

Apart from orchids, it was his first gift to her:
a silver neck-chain, box-linked, hidden in an Easter Egg.
She almost threw it with the wrapper; wore it often.

Next, before she went away, a simple wooden figure
blank but for dark grain running head to foot.
He hoped it worked some kind of voodoo.

Later came soft toys: a cheap bear on a swing;
Snoopy, firmly stuffed with sawdust, a coat
so white even to hold it might have left a mark.

Today the chain is lost; the wooden man
has one broken foot and teeters on the dresser;
the bear hangs sun-paled by a window at the in-laws;

Snoopy, grown grey and stained by damp,
neck half-broken, is buried in their daughter's toy-box.
Most days he wouldn't think of such things

but in their garden now peonies are in flower,
a colour so deep he can't help but recall the time
he took her dancing and she wore one like it in her hair.

In Passing

Did I mention?
Those May trees wrapped
in sloughed plastic, like a winding sheet?
Or how wind through the trees'
last leaves stirred a rattle of applause?

Were you listening? Could you almost hear
that woodpecker, those acorns falling?

And did I say
how the high-pitched glassy light
of that November morning showed
a changed horizon? Or how it made me feel
translucent and revealed?

And I forgot to add the hours of walking
to no apparent purpose, but...

Forgive me. I confess: that
to have driven through, and stood
in such clarity and glare, have felt
at once a need to smile and hide, was
because of finding you again.

Two Feathers

These feathers are for you.
I found them on the roadside,
dun and plain but still intact
among a swathe of poppies
that shone scarlet under rain clouds.
You could keep them with your bag
of beach-scoured twigs and chattering shells.
But first, hold them upright in a wind:
let your fingers feel the way they want to fly;
close your eyes and think of beating wings;
imagine I am giving you the gift of flight.

Losing Grip

Holding three eggs in one hand, he reads
a long letter written in a little space;
moves towards a battered stool and sits
slowly, actions well rehearsed, knowing
where the seat will be, where to rest his arm.

Outside a horse is being broken; taught
to trot in circles, hubbed by rein and stick.
A tall girl tugs and guides, clicks her tongue
and talks as if to stop the brute complaining.

He doesn't hear the words – only reads again
of how his daughter won't be coming,
how it isn't anything he's done
but what with work, the kids, the cost
of flying, she cannot manage any more.

He takes deep breaths, shuts his eyes
to picture her: there beneath the sun; here
in plaits, an age ago, cycling round the lawn.
One egg falls from his slackened grip.

At Littleborough

I am reading the names.
Bright-clothed strangers emerge into sunlight
from dark lanes by the river
and pass the churchyard,
but I am drawn again to a woman
who died young two kings ago.

And I always picture a flawless face,
the high lace neck of her long dress
which tugs across dry grass;
then someone is calling and waving in the distance
but she does not hear or see, twirling her parasol
against the early evening and motionless trees.
When a boat slips by, its bow waves
push to her the water's scent.

'*Here lies Mary Reckless....*', her bones
wrapped in clay, in darkness.
I see my shadow on the chapel wall;
feel the lych-gate wood against my palm;
listen, just once, to my breathing –
and today it is enough to have done nothing
but outlive her by eight years.

And have I travelled...

...the road to this Jerusalem to find
a cold, reluctant village by a stand of poplars,
the air too strong with vegetable decay
to stay, enjoy the scene; the place
more like a wilderness – windswept, lifeless, silent?

The things that pass for temples here
do not have golden domes or supplicants at prayer.
Here is a place of other, simpler faiths
like what the season's weather holds, not words
that scorched the stubble of an older world.

This is just a hidden corner of a later one:
small farms, combed fields, some pheasant;
people out at work, or inside painted homes
living out the aftermath in ways they've tried
to choose, making do the best they can.